STOCK MARKET INVESTING FOR BEGINNERS

25 GOLDEN INVESTING LESSONS + PROVEN STRATEGIES

MARK ATWOOD

Legal & Disclaimer

The information contained in this book and its contents is not designed to replace or take the place of any form of medical or professional advice; and is not meant to replace the need for independent medical, financial, legal or other professional advice or services, as may be required. The content and information in this book have been provided for educational and entertainment purposes only.

The content and information contained in this book have been compiled from sources deemed reliable, and it is accurate to the best of the Author's knowledge, information, and belief. However, the Author cannot guarantee its accuracy and validity and cannot be held liable for any errors and/or omissions. Further, changes are periodically made to this book as and when needed. Where appropriate and/or necessary, you must consult a professional (including but not limited to your doctor, attorney, financial advisor or such other professional advisor) before using any of the suggested remedies, techniques, or information in this book.

Upon using the contents and information contained in this book, you agree to hold harmless the Author from and against any damages, costs, and expenses, including any legal fees potentially resulting from the application of any of the information provided by this book. This disclaimer applies to any loss, damages or injury caused by the use and application,

CONTENTS

PART: I - STOCK MARKET INVESTING
ESSENTIALS

1. Investing   9
2. Stock Market   17
3. Mutual Funds   21
4. Exchange Traded Funds (ETFs)   31
5. Initial public offerings (IPOs)   36

PART: II - STOCK RESEARCH AND ANALYSIS TO
PICK BEST STOCKS

6. Fundamental Analysis   45
7. Industry Research   51
8. Company Research   57
9. Stock Research   61
10. Financial Statements Analysis   73

PART: III - STRATEGIES TO WIN ON THE STOCK
MARKET

11. Investment Styles and Strategies   93
12. Value Investing   101
13. Growth Investing   105
14. Income Investing   108
15. Stock Market Tips & Tricks   111

PART: IV - ADVANCE STOCK MARKET
STRATEGIES AND TACTICS

16. Short Selling   119
17. Buying on Margin   122
18. Day Trading   125
19. Online Trading   128
20. Portfolio Management   131

PART: V - STOCK MARKET PRACTICAL LESSONS

21. Stock Brokers   137
22. Successful Stock Market Investors   140
23. Stock Market Gurus   145
24. Stock Market and Investment Books   148
25. Stock Market Terminology   152

    Final words   156

PART: I - STOCK MARKET INVESTING ESSENTIALS

1

INVESTING

Investing is one of the greatest tools for creating wealth, particularly if you invest smartly and wisely. Though investments are known to generate massive wealth, it is not for the elite only. Even a person with a modest income can become a great investor with the right strategies and tactics to capitalize on the stock market opportunities.

Before investing in any kind of stocks, you need to change the way you look at the whole idea of investing. You need a new point of view. No matter what kind of thoughts or opinions you have on investing, you must change your mindset and look at investing as a major opportunity.

Being able to buy a part of a company and receive a

portion of their profits as dividends is an incredible opportunity.

The 25 lessons presented in this book will guarantee to give you a head start in your investing career. Make sure to go through each lesson and absorb as much of the knowledge as you can!

Millions of dollars, even billions in some cases, have been made through investing in stock markets even by regular people with limited resources.

The greatest investor in the world, Warren Buffet, was working as a salaried employee in sales and had very limited resources at the beginning of his amazing investing career. The most important part of Warren Buffet's investing career was that he had a very sound strategy from the very beginning and was a devoted disciple of the great investment gurus like Benjamin Graham. Buffet also developed a great sense for picking the best stocks and had the patience to allow his stocks to gain enormous value over time.

You can do the same and generate much money by investing in stock markets. But, you'll need to adopt a well thought out strategy and a sound investment plan.

You can build a fortune by investing in stocks and easily if you start early and capitalize on the miracle of compounding.

You earn money from your job or profession, but it has a severe problem.

You earn money through your job or profession by undertaking it five days a week, however, on the day when you don't show up, you don't earn a single penny. Making money through a day job is active income. If you are not actively working, you do not have an income. It's as simple as that.

The secret behind creating enormous wealth through investing is mainly earning money without any or little active work involved. If you invest in stocks, you become a part-owner of a business. This business keeps on producing money, without you having to do anything in particular. This is what you call passive income.

PASSIVE INCOME! Yes, passive income is the key to enormous wealth creation. Passive income simply explained is putting in the majority of the work once and then have a steady flow of cash for months, years and sometimes even decades with a just a little of maintenance work from time to time. This way of earning an income gives you more time to build additional passive income streams, and this will, in turn, make you more and more money over time. A day job, however, is purely trading your time for a certain amount of money without any opportunity of scaling up. There are a ton of different methods to earn passive income; however, in this book, we cover only stock market investing.

The trick is to start as early as possible. Investing takes time and effort. It is not a method to get rich quick - unless you're lucky, but we're not here to gamble. You can learn a lot about choosing the right investments in this book, and make considerable profits in stocks by judicious use of the various strategies, tactics, and tips.

There are numerous ways to start investing, even with a small sum of money. Technology has made it easy and profitable for small investors to make money in stock markets. You can get information about various investment opportunities easily in today's online digital world.

You need to assess your investment goals and cash needs while investing. You need to determine your liquidity needs along with timing, risk-bearing capacity, the total amount of the investible funds at your disposal, etc.

Investing starts with deciding where you want to invest. You can invest in any one of the assets you prefer. There are a number of asset classes for your investments. The major asset classes are:

- Stocks or equities
- Bonds or Fixed Rate Instruments
- Gold and other commodities
- Real Estate
- Cash or Cash Equivalents
- Alternative Investments like Artwork

Each of the above asset classes has its characteristics, along with its pros and cons. You can decide on one or more asset classes for your investments, taking into account their advantages and disadvantages.

The various asset classes are as follows:

Stocks:

Stocks allow you to become part-owner of a business. You get all the rewards as well as bear the risk.

You get to benefit from dividend and capital appreciation of your stocks.

The company doesn't need to give dividends. Thus, you may not get steady cash flow from your stock investments. So, you may need some supplementary investments in other asset classes, which give a steady or pre-determined cash flow at regular intervals.

Over a long period of time, the stocks tend to edge out other asset classes and provide the best returns.

Bonds or Fixed Rate Instruments:

Bonds give a fixed income per year to you as per the coupon rate. Bonds can also have some increase or decrease in value, depending on interest rates mainly and on credit risk to some extent. It is less risky as compared to stocks.

Gold and Other Commodities:

You can also invest in gold and other commodities; however, the profit you'll make here is only in price increases. Gold and other commodities don't generate an income through any productive activities. Gold taps on the fear factor and increases in value, particularly in case of any political or economic crisis. Commodities also increase in value due to scarcity or disruption in their production.

Real Estate:

You can invest in real estate, residential properties, or land. Almost all wealthy people have an investment in real estate or other properties. Your profits here are in the form of capital appreciation, rent etc.

Cash or Cash Equivalents:

You can keep your investible funds in cash or cash equivalents like checking accounts, saving accounts, money market instruments, etc. They give you very little return. However, you need to keep some of your savings or wealth in cash to meet your liquidity needs or day to day expenses.

Your checking account gives no or negligible return. Your savings account provides a very nominal return, which is not even able to offset the inflation rate. This will reduce your wealth in the long run in real terms. Therefore, you'll need investment options which are at least enough to offset the erosion of your wealth caused by inflation.

Alternative Investments

Nowadays, some people are investing in alternative

assets like artworks, paintings, etc. This is a good investment avenue only for those with sound technical expertise in the particular art or field. There have been cases of fake paintings, turning millions of dollars into dirt. The market is limited and lacks liquidity. If you need cash urgently, it may be difficult to sell off your alternative investments quickly.

Asset Allocation:

You'll need to have a proper asset allocation by dividing your investments among the various asset classes as per your specific needs and circumstances. The asset allocation strategy also depends on your life stage.

People invest more in stocks during their early and stable career. People invest more in fixed-rate instruments as they approach their retirement. This is as per the evolving needs, e.g., more steady income required from your investments when you are not getting a salary or a regular income.

You'll need, however, to have diversified investments - spread across stocks, bonds, cash, etc. - at any point in time in your life.

2

STOCK MARKET

The first step in successful stock market investing is to understand the stock market. This is a very crucial step in your investing journey. If you start investing in the stock market without having a thorough or at least a good understanding of the stock market itself, you may suffer losses in the beginning. These initial losses may discourage you from lifelong stock market investments. So, it is of high importance that you start your journey fully prepared.

A stock market is basically a marketplace to buy and sell stocks of companies. It refers collectively to all the stock exchanges, where the issuing and trading of stocks take place. Stock trading can be done on the proper exchange platform or an over-the-counter market. The stock market is also referred to as the equity market. The stock market provides a company with a mechanism to get capital from investors in lieu of partial or fractional ownership.

The stock market has two main parts viz. primary market and secondary market. The new issues of the stocks are sold in the primary market by the company going public. The subsequent buying and selling of the stock, after it has been listed and sold by the company, takes place in the secondary market.

Stock Exchanges:

Stock exchanges have been established in all major financial centers and cities across the world, such as New York, London, Hong Kong, Singapore, Tokyo, etc.

New York Stock Exchange (NYSE) and the NASDAQ are the two largest stock exchanges in the United States. NYSE was founded in 1792. NYSE is the biggest stock exchange in the world in terms of market capitalization.

Stock Market Risks:

There are a number of risks associated with stock

market investing. The volatility of stock prices is one of the most critical risks associated with investing in stocks. The rise and decline in the price of stock even by 20% in a day, is not a matter of surprise.

Sometimes, there is a widespread decline or fall in the prices of almost all the stocks. This situation is known as a stock market crash and is very painful to the stockholders. In case of a stock market crash, the investors may not find any buyers for many of the stocks they hold.

Regulators of the Stock Markets:

Governments of many countries have established regulators to monitor the activities of the stock exchanges with an aim to protect investors.

In the US, the Securities and Exchange Commission (SEC) is the primary regulator that monitors the US stock markets. The SEC outlines that its mission is to protect investors, maintain fair, orderly, and efficient markets, and facilitate capital formation."

Stock Market Functionaries and Players:

The stock market has many functionaries and players. They are stockbrokers, traders, portfolio managers, stock analysts, and investment bankers. They have different roles to play but are interrelated.

Stockbrokers buy and sell securities on behalf of the investors. Portfolio managers look after and manage the investments or stocks for their clients. Stock analysts research stocks and rate them for buying and selling. Investment bankers work for the companies for their IPOs, mergers, and acquisitions, etc.

3

MUTUAL FUNDS

One of the safer methods of investing in stocks is investing in mutual funds. Mutual funds invest in stocks as well; however, they pool the investible funds of a large number of investors and then invest that collective pool of funds on the individual stocks. If there is any loss in one particular stock, it is spread over a large number of investors, and consequently, the loss to an individual investor is quite bearable. This is simply due to the large magnitude of the total stocks. Therein dwells the beauty of investing in stocks through mutual funds.

The benefit of diversification, which is not available to a small investor in pure stock investing, becomes available to the smallest individual investor thanks to mutual funds. The mutual fund companies, also known as asset management companies, employ professionally qualified and experienced persons to manage the investments. Their expertise and professional approach to stock investing serve the small investors very well; thus, mutual funds are an effective, efficient, and less risky way to invest in the stocks. However, mutual funds are not a totally risk-free way of investing. Mutual funds also include various fees and expenses. The investor has to bear them ultimately.

Advantages of Mutual Funds:

- **Diversification:** Mutual funds have well-diversified portfolios. They have a large number of stocks of numerous companies across many industries. This helps them in bearing the risk due to a sudden or large loss caused by a particular stock or industry. By spreading the investments across the spectrum of stocks, companies, or industries, you can protect your investments in the times of wide swings or market fluctuations. Mutual funds are a real-life application of an age-old maxim "Don't put all your eggs in one basket."
- **Variety:** The mutual funds, particularly the

large and well established mutual funds, have an enormous amount of money to invest, and this means that they can invest in an array of assets and asset classes. For example, some mutual funds may invest in a mix of large caps and mid caps. The large caps give stability to the portfolio, while mid caps provide the growth potential.

- **Affordability:** If investors want to build a well-diversified portfolio, they will need a considerable amount to invest. But, a small investor can also invest in a well-diversified portfolio through a mutual fund by placing an affordable amount.
- **Dividend:** You can earn a steady income through dividends declared and distributed by the mutual fund.
- **Liquidity:** You can also redeem your mutual fund portfolio at the net asset value (NAV).
- **Professional Expertise:** Mutual funds are managed by people with a lot of financial expertise and experience. This makes it easier for you to reap the benefits of well-chosen investments.

Disadvantages of Mutual Funds:

- **Costs:** You have to bear ultimately all the costs, fees, and charges related to the operations of the mutual fund or the asset management company. This reduces the value of your mutual fund portfolio or the net asset value (NAV) as well as the returns. You have to bear these costs even if the performance of the mutual fund is negative i.e.; you have made losses with the decline in the total value of your mutual fund portfolio.
- **Risk of Loss:** You have all the risks related to stock investing when you invest in a mutual fund. You may lose a part or all of your money in a mutual fund investment in case of market volatility.
- **Performance:** Though the mutual funds have a past performance and track record, it does not make sure that the future performance would be outstanding.
- **Limited Potential:** When markets are on the move with high growth in selected stocks or industries, you may not gain the full profit potential of investing in those specific stocks or industries. This is because your investments are in a diversified mutual fund.
- **Lack of Guarantee:** Mutual fund

investments are not guaranteed by the government or by any other government agency like the guarantee you have for your deposits in the bank in many countries, e.g., the guarantee of Federal Deposit Insurance Corporation (FDIC) in the US.

You can decide on whether or not to invest your money in mutual funds after considering the advantages and disadvantages of the mutual funds in your individual case, taking into account your investment objectives, size of portfolio, risk appetite, etc.

Types of Mutual Funds

There are various types of mutual funds in which you can invest. Mutual funds have three main categories viz. stock funds or equity funds, bond funds, and money market funds. Each category of mutual funds has its unique features, returns, and risks. Higher the return potential, the higher is the risk of loss.

There are some restrictions imposed on the mutual fund with respect to where and how much it can invest in the different types of assets or stocks depending on its category. However, these rules vary from country to country. In some countries, some rules require a mutual fund to invest at least 80% in assets belonging to its declared category. You can have an idea of the exact type of investments from the mutual fund prospectus.

Money Market Mutual Funds: These are funds that invest in short-term investments or securities issued by the government, or creditworthy leading corporates. They are less volatile as compared to the other types of mutual funds. But, they have low returns also. The returns usually move in tandem with the short-term interest rates. They offer a good alternative to keeping your money in cash in a bank account, as they provide high liquidity i.e., you can cash-out quickly.

Bond Mutual Funds: These are funds that invest in the bonds issued by the government and companies. They have higher risks as compared to the money market funds, but less risk as compared to the stock or equity funds. Most of the bond funds focus on higher yields. The bond fund's earnings after expenses are known as bond yield, which mainly depends on bond quality and maturity.

These funds mainly face credit risk, i.e., the risk that the counterparty viz. bond issuing government entity or the company may fail to pay the coupon/interest or the principal amount. The credit risk depends on the quality of the bonds contained in the fund portfolio. These funds also face interest rate risk and usually, the market value of the bond funds goes down when interest rates rise, particularly in case of longer term-bonds. Often, the lower the quality or, the longer the maturity of the bond, the higher is the yield and risk.

Stock or Equity Mutual Funds: These funds invest in stocks of various companies. They have higher risks as compared to money market or bond funds. They also have high volatility. But, the stock or equity mutual funds have performed much better than other investments over the long term historically.

These funds mainly face market risk. The prices of stocks may fluctuate considerably. The prices may fluctuate due to many reasons, e.g., changes in the overall economy, industry-level happenings, individual company or stock level developments, input costs, management changes, etc.

Stock or Equity Mutual Funds is a broad level category and include many sub-categories of mutual funds in it, such as:

- **Growth Funds**: focus on stocks with high growth potential.
- **Income Funds:** focus on stocks paying regular dividends.
- **Sector Funds:** focus on a particular industry or sector, e.g., IT, telecom, etc.
- **Index Funds:** focus on a portfolio of stocks replicating an Index to achieve the same return, e.g., S&P 500.
- **Balanced Funds**: focus on a portfolio with an optimum combination of both the stocks and bonds.

Buying and Selling of Mutual Funds

You may buy the stocks of mutual funds in a number of ways. The most common way is either buying from the fund itself or buying through a financial advisor.

The price for mutual fund stocks is usually calculated based on the per stock net asset value (NAV) of the mutual fund. Depending on a mutual fund, there may be a stockholder fee imposed at the time of buying, such as sales load. The NAV of a mutual fund is calculated at the end of the particular business day by dividing the total value of the holdings of the mutual fund after deduction of expenses by the total number of stocks owned by the mutual fund. Buyers of mutual funds buy at the NAV calculated after they place the buying order.

The stocks of mutual funds are redeemable, i.e., the investor can sell the stocks back to the mutual fund at any point in time.

All said and done, mutual fund investing is a great and fantastic way to invest in stocks. There are many mutual funds with wide-ranging characteristics, different types of portfolios, and investment philosophies. You may choose the one which best fits your individual needs and circumstances in terms of return objectives, risk tolerance, liquidity needs, etc.

It will allow you to learn about stock investing if you continuously track the performance of your mutual fund portfolio and how it moves with the overall stock markets as well as with the peer group of mutual funds.

Thus, you will start recognizing a pattern of price movements in the stocks with relation to the economic environment, the performance of the industries and businesses, earnings, results of companies, etc. After a while, when you become well versed with all these investment-related things, you may decide to take a plunge in the wide ocean of stock investing on your own; and come out with flying colors.

4

EXCHANGE TRADED FUNDS (ETFS)

E xchange Traded Funds (ETFs) are like traditional mutual funds with an extra facility to the holders to buy and sell them like stocks on the stock exchanges. In other words, it is a type of security and has characteristics similar to the close-ended mutual funds, which are listed on the stock exchanges. ETFs are bought and sold on the stock exchange throughout the trading day just like a stock, and the price changes continuously.

ETFs track an index, a sector, or a commodity like an index fund. ETFs own assets such as stocks, bonds, commodities, etc. The stockholders, who indirectly own the fund assets, get a portion of the profits, interest, or dividends. Some financial institutions buy and redeem ETF stocks and large blocks known as creation units.

ETFs started in 1989 with the Index Participation Stocks, which was an S&P 500 proxy and traded on American Stock Exchange. Standard & Poor's Depositary Receipts (SPDRs) was introduced in 1993, and the fund soon became the largest ETF in the world. Barclays Global Investors launched the iStocks in 2000, which became the largest ETF by 2005. Over the years, ETFs proliferated with various niche ETFs catering to the specific needs related to different sectors, commodities, regions, etc. By 2014, the number of ETFs crossed 1,500 with assets above $2 trillion.

ETFs provide diversification, tax efficiency, and low expense ratio. At the same time, they also provide features of ordinary stock, like limit orders, options, short selling, etc.

Advantages of Exchange Traded Funds (ETFs):

Lesser Costs: ETFs have lesser costs as compared to most of the investment products, as they spend less on marketing, sales, and administrative expenses. This is due to the fact that most of the ETFs are not actively managed, and secondly, they don't spend

much on buying and selling of stocks for accommo-
dating the purchases and redemptions.

Buying and Selling Ease: You can buy or sell ETFs
easily on a stock exchange during the trading day.
You can buy ETF stocks on margin. You can use stop
orders and limit orders specifying the price points.

Tax Efficiency: ETFs are tax efficient as they have a
low turnover of portfolio securities, and don't need
to sell securities to meet redemptions.

Diversification: ETFs have a diversified portfolio
and provide you diversification across a full index,
industry, sector, etc.

Transparency: ETFs have transparent portfolios.
Moreover, their prices are set at frequent intervals
during a trading day.

Types of Exchange Traded Funds (ETFs):

Index ETFs

Most of the ETFs are index funds and replicate the
performance of a particular index. The index can be
based on stocks, commodities, bonds, etc. The index
ETFs invest proportionately in accordance with the
underlying securities in an index.

Stock ETFs:

Many ETFs track stocks and some index like the S&P 500. Stock ETFs have different styles like large-cap, mid-cap, etc. ETFs may be a sector fund, e.g., IT or banking. It can be global or country-specific. Thus, you can have many options while investing in an ETF.

Bond ETFs:

Many ETFs invest in bonds like government treasury bonds, blue-chip company bonds, etc. These are excellent investment options during a recession, as the stocks don't perform well in such times.

Commodity ETFs:

There are ETFs that invest in commodities, e.g., precious metals like gold, other metals like copper, agricultural produce, etc. Many commodity ETFs are index funds that track some non-security index. These are riskier as compared to other ETFs, as the commodity prices are affected by many factors and also due to speculative activities.

Currency ETFs:

Some ETFs invest in currencies of different countries such as USD, GBP, EUR, etc. They track a single currency or a basket of major currencies. These are very volatile due to the extreme volatility of the underlying, i.e., currencies.

You can pick ETFs based on your investment objectives and individual needs. You should buy an ETF, which gives you the desired risk-reward ratio. You should try to buy an ETF with a good track record, low expenses, low tracking error, etc.

Exchange Traded Funds (ETFs) are a very good option for investing. You can buy and sell ETFs like stocks, and also go short. You can get the diversification of the mutual funds with the versatility of a stock. ETF investment is like buying an entire portfolio of stocks as if you are buying a single stock.

5

INITIAL PUBLIC OFFERINGS (IPOS)

Initial public offering (IPO) refers to the sale of stocks to the public for the first time by a newly formed or hitherto private company. A private company has a minimal number of stockholders, and those are usually the founders, their relatives, and friends. Sometimes, however, there are some professional investors like angel investors and venture capitalists, who invest in private companies. They can also borrow from banks but, usually, the pool of investible resources remains very limited for a private company. Therefore, private companies or newly formed companies like to go public to tap the vast resources in terms of investible funds. IPO is the first step in this direction.

Primary Market:

The primary market is the marketplace for the first offering of stocks by a company. The company gets money directly from the public in its own coffers in exchange for shares of the company. It is different from the secondary market, where the company stocks are traded among the people, and money changes hands between the two involved public parties without any money coming to the company. In the primary market, investors buy stocks from the company itself.

Initial public offerings (IPOs):

Public companies may have tens of thousands of investors who have bought the stocks of the company; therefore, the public companies are subject to rigorous strict rules and regulations. Public companies must form a board of directors, including independent directors. Public companies must also report their accounts and financial information periodically and timely. A public company must submit its records to a government or public regulator of the country in which it is registered. For example, in the US, public companies report and submit records to the Securities and Exchange Commission (SEC)

A public company should also comply with the rules

and regulations of the stock exchanges on which its stocks are listed. Listing on a well-known stock exchange such as NYSE brings much repute and gives a boost to the company image along with other benefits. Only private companies with solid fundamentals can qualify for an IPO and a listing on a reputed stock exchange.

Reasons for IPO:

When a private company goes public and brings an IPO, it gets an opportunity to raise a large amount of money for its various needs, including future expansion. For example, the American Insurance Group (AIG) raised $20.5 billion in 2006, and Alibaba Group (BABA) raised $25 billion in 2014.

Once a private company brings an IPO and becomes a publicly traded company, it achieves greater public trust due to the auditing and public scrutiny of its accounts and records. Public companies are also able to get loans from banks and financial institutions at a lower rate and can issue debt instruments to the public at better terms.

They can also issue more stock to the public in a secondary offering. They can issue stock to part-finance mergers and acquisitions. If you buy stock in an IPO of a company going public, you may sell your shares in the secondary market, which is the market for resale and purchase of stocks among the public. Sometimes, the stocks see a huge boost in their prices post listing, which can lead to a huge profit if you decide to sell your stocks on the secondary market.

Advantages and Disadvantages of an IPO:

Advantages:

- The company can tap a vast number of investors to raise the required capital.
- The company gets funds at a lower cost.
- The public image and reputation of the company get a very significant boost.
- The increase in the public image also helps a company in increasing its sales.
- The company can attract a better workforce by offering stock options.
- The company can use its stock for financing the mergers and acquisitions.
- The company can raise enormous funds for the company as compared to any other option like a bank loan.
- The company has a low-risk fund, as the

company is not required to pay dividends to the stockholders at any fixed rate or periodicity.

Disadvantages:

- A private company, after going public, has to disclose its accounts and all important information to the public.
- The company has to incur various legal, accounting, and other costs. Many of these costs have to incur on a regular basis after going public.
- The company founders, owners, or management have to devote much time and effort to fulfill many reporting and compliance requirements.
- Risk of not getting a proper response from the public and not being able to raise the required amount of funding.
- The public information, particularly the crucial business or operational information, may be used by the competitors to gain an advantage over the company.
- IPO leads to loss of control from the

founders or owners of the company management and its affairs.

- The new public stockholders get voting rights and thus get the power to control or even delay/hamper decisions through the board of directors

- The company faces increased risks regarding legal and regulatory issues like class-action lawsuits.

An IPO also serves as an exit route for the founders of the company as well as the early investors in the company, such as angel investors, venture capitalists, etc. They get rewarded and make profits for risk-taking by investing in the company in its nascent stage. However, the owners often keep a significant portion of the total stock, and sometimes a majority stock to maintain their control over the company, even after an IPO.

Investing in IPOs:

IPOs have proven to be a jackpot for some investors. But, at the same time, they carry very high risk; as you are investing in an unknown and little-scrutinized company.

You should invest in an IPO with solid fundamentals. You should dig deep into the founders and company management. You can analyze the business model, the production capacity, total investment of the founders/owners, etc.

When you are well satisfied with your analysis of the company, you should go ahead with investing in the IPO of the company. But, never invest in an IPO based on the market hype or social media buzz.

PART: II - STOCK RESEARCH AND ANALYSIS TO PICK BEST STOCKS

6

FUNDAMENTAL ANALYSIS

Fundamental analysis is highly important to analyze stocks properly. It focuses on understanding and calculating the intrinsic value of a particular stock. It is based on an in-depth and comprehensive analysis of the numerous economic, financial, and business factors and variables. The various factors affecting the value of a stock are analyzed on the basis of their nature, i.e., qualitative and quantitative factors.

Fundamental analysis observes macroeconomic trends and industry-specific factors as well as the several elements that affect the stock prices such as sales, gross profit, net profit, debt, earnings per stock (EPS), price to earnings (P/E) ratio, etc.

There are two approaches to fundamental analysis viz. top-down approach and bottom-up approach.

Top-down Approach :

- First of all, the entire stock market is analyzed. You consider all the macroeconomic indicators like GDP growth rate, industrial production, interest rates in the domestic economy, inflation rate, unemployment rate, housing prices, overall market trends, etc. You may also include the relevant global indicators like the growth of the world economy, global commodity prices, export growth rate, etc.
- You, then, analyze a particular sector of your interest—for example, transport.
- Thereafter, you study and analyze the specific industry, say the car manufacturing industry.
- Ultimately, you analyze a particular stock such as General Motors. You consider the various stock level factors like sales, net profit, return on equity (ROE), return on assets (ROA), input prices, company financial statements, etc. You'll also need to

analyze the prices of related factors like crude oil prices, the activities of the competitors like Ford motors, the emerging threats like Tesla, etc.

Bottom-up approach - it has just the opposite direction, and begins with the analysis of the particular stock and ends with the analysis of the economy level factors.

You may follow any of the two approaches, but the objective remains the same, i.e., finding out the true value of a stock. This enables you to compare the true value with the current market price to determine whether a particular stock is undervalued or overvalued. Once you have arrived at the valuation of a stock, you can take your buying or selling decision, i.e., sell the overvalued stock and buy the undervalued stock.

Fundamental Analysis Tools:

Company Reports - Most of the information that you need for fundamental analysis is available in various reports of the company, particularly the annual report. You may download company reports from the company website free of charge.

Macro Economy Trends and Analysis - You'll need information and data related to the macroeconomy and the trends. If the macroeconomy data and trends point to an overall downturn, then you should wait before buying any stock as stock prices may fall in the coming days. If the economic variables and data indicate a bleak outlook for a particular industry, avoid buying stocks pertaining to that industry.

Industry Information - You will need industry information to determine how the company is performing as compared to its peers in the industry. You'll also need the data for analyzing the current performance and future prospects of the industry as a whole. You may get some useful information and data free of cost from the website of the industry's association.

Latest Developments and News Updates - You can find a lot of useful information regarding the latest developments and happenings which are relevant for forming a perspective on the company or stock in a good business newspaper or a magazine like WSJ and NYT. You may take advantage of business news websites for keeping track of the latest developments related to the industry or the stock of your interest. You may get information and old-time series data from the archives of a good business news site like yahoo finance, MSN money, etc.

Software and Apps - You would need software like spreadsheet programs for doing some analysis or calculations at your end. You may use MS Excel for many useful fundamental calculations. You may take advantage of various handy mobile apps that can help you in the process of tracking stocks.

The Significance of Fundamental Analysis:

Fundamental analysis is a holistic method to analyze a stock or a business. Fundamental analysis looks at the complete picture by studying and analyzing all the possible movements in the stock market as well as in the individual stocks.

If you wish to invest for the long term, it is essential to understand the particular stock along with the business of the company from various angles. It is critical that you can separate the short-term noise in price movements of a stock and the overall stock market from the underlying business performance of the company.

The price of the stock of a fundamentally strong company tends to appreciate in the long term. It creates much wealth for investors, e.g., Microsoft. The fundamental analysis has been used very successfully by numerous investors, including all-time great Warren Buffett.

7

INDUSTRY RESEARCH

Industry research is a very vital component of the fundamental analysis that you undertake for analyzing the stocks of your investments. Each and every industry has its own unique features and characteristics which make it different from other industries. Consequently, each industry needs a specific analysis.

You'll need to analyze the industry structure, the number of firms in the industry, customer base, market share of different firms, industry growth, internal competition among the firms in the industry as well as the external competition with other industries, rules and regulations governing the industry, the life cycle of the industry, etc. The analysis and understanding of the industry along the lines mentioned above would give you a much deeper understanding and perspective on the company's current financial health and prospects.

Industry Growth:

You need to analyze the growth of the industry in order to zero in on the right industry for your investments. In a high growth industry, most of the firms have good chances not only to earn high profits but also to grow at a rapid pace. This will always be beneficial for you in view of your investments in the company belonging to the industry.

You may judge the growth potential of the industry by assessing the fact whether the total revenues of the industry are growing or whether the number of customers of the industry is increasing. If it is so, you may invest in the companies of this industry.

If revenue is not growing, and customers are not increasing, there would be intense rivalry among the firms in the industry. This may have negative outcomes like cut-throat competition, price wars, and companies trying to snatch market share from each other. Ideally, you should avoid investing in such an industry.

Competition

It is of paramount importance that you analyze the competitive landscape of the industry. There are some industries, which have no or minimal barriers to entry. This leads to a large number of firms competing for the same customers in the market and a harsh operating environment for the companies in the industry.

The intensive competition in an industry reduces pricing power of the companies, and ability to pass on the cost increases. It often leads to price wars, reducing the profits of the companies. You should avoid such an industry.

On the other hand, less intense competition is very beneficial for the firms in the industry. If you invest in the stock of a company of such an industry, you stand to make a profit from your stock investments in the future.

Market Share:

Market share is an important metric to analyze while evaluating stock investments. The market share of a company tells you about the strength of a company. If the company has a significant market share, it will have some pricing power over the customers. Moreover, it also suggests that the company has some competitive advantages. It may also be due to some type of entry barriers of that industry.

Thus, a company with a large market share is a better bet for your investment because you may get good dividends and capital appreciation from your stocks in such a company. If the company is a market leader in the industry; it is a better option for your investment, as it will enjoy economies of scale and earn more profits.

Customer Base:

The customer base is one of the most important fundamentals for the long-term success of a company. Many companies have a small number of customers, while other companies have millions. So, you'll need to analyze the customer base of a company in the context of its industry and its peer group. Usually, if a company has only a small number of customers, it is a sign of weakness. For example, if a railway equipment supplier has 100% of its sales to the government railway monopoly company in a country, a single change in government policy may cause it to lose all the sales revenue overnight.

In similar industries like defense production, aircraft, and petroleum machinery, etc., the customer base is small. Thus, you need to analyze the industry and peers to judge whether the company has a sufficient number of customers. However, you would be better off investing in the stocks of a company that has a large customer base.

Regulation

There are some industries that are heavily regulated owing to their importance for the public at large; for example, drug industry, banking, utilities, etc. Regulating such industries is very crucial for public welfare, but it increases their risk and reduces their pricing power. This reduces their profit prospects. Your investments in such industries have limited profit potential and an unattractive risk-reward ratio.

Moreover, you should carefully watch out for any new regulations which may affect an industry drastically. New strict regulations reduce the future prospects of a company and may have a severe impact on the market prices of their stocks. If you have invested in the stocks of such industries, you may have to suffer losses in the short and medium-term.

Therefore, you should keep the regulatory costs in mind when you assess the stocks and industries for investing.

8

COMPANY RESEARCH

Every single piece of stock represents fractional ownership in a specific company. The company is the legal entity around which everything related to stock investing revolves. If a company fails, your investments in the stocks of that particular company are going to turn to junk.

In view of this fundamental aspect of stock investing, it is of paramount importance that you do research specifically about the company, its business model, management, etc. You need to understand the qualitative aspects of the company.

Business Model

The business model basically refers to what a company does or how a company earns money. In some cases, the business model of a company is quite easy to understand. For example, Pizza Hut sells pizzas of different types along with certain related foods and drinks, earns revenue from the customers, and after deducting its expenses, earns a profit.

The company is going to earn revenue and profits as long as people like to eat pizzas, and the company can serve them attractive pizza offerings with value for money at reasonable operational costs. You must understand the cost drivers and the future drivers of growth and profit for a particular company.

Warren Buffett seldom invests in the companies which he doesn't understand.

Competitive Advantage

A company's continued success is based on its ability to maintain a competitive advantage or edge over its competitors. For example, Microsoft has a tremendous competitive advantage as Windows dominates more than 80% of the operating system market in the world. This not only gives it an edge over its competitors in the operating system arena but also provides an excellent launchpad for its other application software like MS Office. Consequently, Microsoft can make great profits. It is also on a firm footing to achieve future growth and profits for the stockholders.

Company Management

The management team of the company is a crucial aspect to be considered while evaluating a company. It is the management that leads a company to success. You can judge the management from the information provided on the corporate website, annual report, particularly Management Discussion and Analysis (MD&A) section, and also from inter-actions during conference calls and company presentations.

You can assess the management on the basis of past performance and corporate governance. You can also judge the outlook of the management from ownership and insider sales information.

A competent and stable management team is a boon for a company and would go a long way in ensuring high-level performance of the company. Such a company is a good candidate for investments.

Corporate Governance

You should also examine the corporate governance practices of the company. Corporate governance refers to the policies which ensure that there are proper checks and balances to prevent unethical and illegal activities. Good corporate governance is necessary for safekeeping of the interests of the investors in the company.

Good corporate governance focuses on the following:

There is financial and information transparency in the company with good quality and timely financial disclosures.

The company policies should benefit and secure the stockholder interests. If a company gives the stock-holders voting rights to call meetings to discuss crucial issues with the company board, it is plus for your stock investments.

If the board of directors has an equal combination inside and outside directors, it helps in serving the interests of the stockholders. The board of directors should have a fair degree of independence. If there are more independent directors on the board of directors, you can consider investing in the stocks of the company favorably.

9

STOCK RESEARCH

Y ou invest in particular stocks; therefore, you'll need to find specific information related to that particular stock before making your investment in it

All the publicly traded stocks are listed on one or the other stock exchange. Stock exchanges assign a unique ticker symbol to each individual stock for identification purposes. You'll need to know the ticker symbol of a stock if you want to research the stock, get a quote, and when placing trade orders.

The term stock ticker denotes the long-outdated telegraph machine. During 1870-1970, the telegraph machine was used to print abbreviated company symbols and the prices of their stocks on the paper tape. Of late, the old scrolling paper tickers have been replaced almost everywhere by the electronic display boards or digital crawls on the financial TV channels and websites.

The stock ticker symbol is generally one to five letters long. Sometimes, the stock ticker contains a hyphen or period to designate a different type or class of stocks. A number of the oldest and biggest companies have a stock ticker with only one single letter stock symbol; for example, Citigroup has 'C', and Ford Motor Company has 'F' as their stock ticker.

Most of the stock exchanges and stock related websites allow you to search for information related to a stock based on its ticker.

For example, in Yahoo Finance, if you enter the ticker WMT for Wal-Mart Stock Quote, you'll get the Wal-Mart stock related information as shown below:

From the above stock information and chart, you can get several details related to Wal-Mart, such as stock prices at close, previous close, open, etc. The details and implications of the various types of information are given below for your benefit.

- Last Price at Close: It refers to the price at which the stock traded at the time of the closing of the trading at the stock exchange. In the above chart, the last price for the Wal-Mart stock is $87.44 at the closing of the trading of the stock on the stock exchange at 4:00 PM EDT.

- Today's Change: It refers to the change in the price of the particular stock. The increase in the closing price of the stock today as compared to the closing price of the stock on the previous trading day is shown in green color, while the decline is shown in red color usually. In the above chart, the price of Wal-Mart stock has shown an increase of $1.04.

- Today's Percentage Change: It refers to the percentage change in the price of the particular stock. The percentage increase in the closing price of the stock today as compared to the closing price of the stock on the previous trading day is shown in green color, while the decline is shown in red color usually. In the above chart, the price of Wal-Mart stock has shown a percentage increase of 1.20%.

- After Hours Last Price: It refers to the price at which the stock traded at the time of the closing of after-hours trading at the stock exchange. In the above chart, the after-hours last price for the Wal-Mart stock is $87.38 at the closing of the trading of the stock on the stock exchange at 6:20 PM EDT. In the above chart, the after-hours price for Wal-Mart stock is $87.38.

- After Hours Change: It refers to the after-hours change in the price of the particular stock. The price of Wal-Mart stock has shown an after-hours decrease of $0.06.

- After Hours Percentage Change: It refers to the after-hours percentage change in the price of the particular stock. The price of Wal-Mart stock has shown an after-hours percentage decrease of 0.07%.

- Previous Close: It shows the price of a stock for the last trade on the previous day. The previous price for the Wal-Mart stock is $86.40 in the chart shown above.

- Open: It denotes the first price at which a stock traded when the stock markets opened up in the morning today. You should be aware that a stock does not open at the same price that it closed on the day before. The open price for the Wal-Mart stock is $86.60.

- Bid: The bid price is the highest price, which a particular buyer is currently willing to pay for the specific stock. The bid price for the Wal-Mart stock is $87.38.

- Ask: The asking price is the lowest price for the stock at which a seller is currently willing to sell the stock. The asking price is also known as the offer price. The ask price for the Wal-Mart stock is $87.44.

- Size: It indicates the number of stocks for the bid or the asking price. The size of the Wal-Mart stock is 200.

- Day's Range: It shows the range of prices in which the stock has traded during the trading day on the stock exchange. It has two price points - the highest price which the stock traded and the lowest price at which the stock traded of the day. The day's range for the Wal-Mart stock is $86.28 - 87.45.

- 52 Week Range: It shows the range of prices in which the stock has traded during the last 52 weeks on the stock exchange. It has two price points - the highest price at which the stock was traded and the lowest price at which the stock was traded during the last 52 weeks. The 52-week range for the Wal-Mart stock is $65.28 - $87.45.

- 52 Week High: It is the highest price at

which the stock has traded during the last 52 weeks. Thus, you can compare the current price to its 52-week range to make a guess about its valuation - whether it is overvalued or undervalued.

The 52 week high for the Wal-Mart stock is $87.45. Thus, it is obvious that the current stock price of Wal-Mart is almost at the level of 52 week high. In such a situation, many of the stock investors would like to avoid investing in the stock, considering it in the overvalued territory.

- 52 Week Low: It is the lowest price at which the stock has traded during the last 52 weeks. Thus, you can compare the current price of the stock to its 52-week range to make a guess about its valuation - whether it is overvalued or undervalued at the current price. The 52 week low for the Wal-Mart stock is $65.28.
- Volume: It indicates the number of stocks that have traded today. Some stocks may have been traded in millions of stocks on a day, but other stocks may have only been traded in a few hundred or even zero stocks on a particular

day. Avg. Volume indicates the average traded volume of the Wal-Mart stock. The volume for the Wal-Mart stock is 7,616,760.

- Market Cap: It refers to the market capitalization of the stock. It is based on the current market price of the stock and the total number of stocks on the company. The market capitalization of Wal-Mart is $261.20 billion on the current stock price.

- Beta: Beta is a very important indicator for stock investors. It is a measure of the volatility of a specific stock as compared to the stock market as a whole. It is symbolized by the Greek letter β.

A stock with a beta of 1 implies that the stock moves in tandem with the stock market, i.e., the price of the stock increases in the same ratio as the increase in the total stock market. Similarly, the price of the stock decreases in the same ratio as the decrease in the total stock market.

A stock with a beta of greater than 1 implies that the stock moves more than the stock market, i.e., the price of the stock increases more than the increase in the total stock market. Similarly, the price of the stock decreases more than the decrease in the total stock market.

A stock with a beta of less than 1 implies that the stock moves less than the stock market, i.e., the price of the stock increases less than the increase in the total stock market. Similarly, the price of the stock decreases less than the decrease in the total stock market. A negative beta for a stock implies that the stock moves in the opposite direction to the stock market.

The beta for the Wal-Mart stock is 0.05. It is positive and implies that the price of the Wal-Mart stock moves in the same direction as the stock market, but it moves less than the market.

- PE Ratio (TTM): It refers to the price to earnings ratio of the trailing twelve months. The PE ratio (TTM) for the Wal-Mart stock is 21.01.
- EPS (TTM): It refers to the earnings per stock of the trailing twelve months. In other words, it is the profit per stock. EPS (TTM) is calculated by dividing the annual profit in the company's most recent year by the

number of stocks outstanding. The EPS (TTM) for the Wal-Mart stock is $4.16.

- Earnings Date: It is the date of the next quarterly results of the company. The earnings date for the Wal-Mart stock is November 16, 2017.

- Forward Dividend: It refers to the expected dividend per stock in the current financial year. Annual dividends are the cash payments which a company makes as a way of return to the stockholders. If you have invested in the stock, you get somewhat regular income in the form of stock dividends. The forward dividend for the Wal-Mart stock is $2.04.

- Forward Dividend Yield: It refers to the expected dividend yield per stock in the current financial year. The annual dividend yield is a very important measure of the return of a stock. It is calculated by dividing the annual dividend amount by the current stock price. If the price of a stock is $20.00 and the company pays out the cash dividend of $3.00, then the stock has an annual dividend yield of 15%. The forward dividend yield for the Wal-Mart stock is 2.57%.

- Ex-Dividend Date: It refers to the cut-off date to be entitled to receive the next dividend payment. If you purchase stock after the ex-dividend date, you will not be able to receive the next dividend payment, which would be received by the seller of the stock. The ex-dividend date for the Wal-Mart stock is November 16, 2017.

- 1y Target Est: It is the estimated price target for the stock for the next year by the market or the analysts. The 1-year target price estimation of the Wal-Mart stock is $86.94.

The current market price of Wal-Mart stock is $87.44. Thus, it is obvious that the current stock price of Wal-Mart is more than a 1-year target estimated for the price of the Wal-Mart stock, which is $86.94. In such a scenario, many of the stock investors would like to avoid investing in the Wal-Mart stock, considering it in the overvalued territory.

If you go to a good website, you'll find that the stock quote listing also includes some stock charts of different types. All these charts track the pricing data of the stock, for example, open, high, low, and close (OHLC) price data of the stock.

You'll find the line charts, bar charts, and the candle-stick charts. You'll also have options for selecting the date ranges, as well as the option to have overlay information such as the volume, moving averages, etc. However, you may not get some of the information in the stock quote, as it is available only to the paid subscribers. In the above chart, you have the option to select the date range 1-day or 5-year for Wal-Mart stock.

Thus, there is a lot of information related to a particular stock in which you are interested. There are a number of sources from which you can obtain this information.

FINANCIAL STATEMENTS ANALYSIS

F inancial Statements are the foundations for all your research and analysis for making investments in the stocks of a company. They are the gold-mine of information related to stock investments. You can pick the gold by analyzing them in detail before committing your money to a stock or company.

Income statement, balance sheet, and cash flow statement are the three most important financial statements.

Income Statement

The income statement is the most important financial statement. It measures the performance of a company over a specific period of time. The preparation of the income statement is usually done quarterly and annually.

The income statement gives information about revenue, expense, and profit generated as a result of the operations of the company during a particular period of time. It also contains the information such as earnings per stock (EPS).

You get to know from the income statement about how much money the company generated, how much money is spent, and how much profit the company made during a particular time period.

You can know from the income statement how well the company is performing and how profitable the business is. A company is fundamentally strong if it has low expenses and lots of sales or revenue simply because this equals more profit. A company like this is worth your investments.

Revenue, also known as sales, represents total money that a company has acquired in a specific time period. The most common and sound way for a company to increase profitability is increasing its sales revenue.

You can judge the quality of a company's revenue on the basis of continuity or sustainability. The temporary increases due to some extraordinary reasons, like the sale of an asset, are not sustainable. Your stock investing decisions should not be based on such revenues.

Income Statement of Wal-Mart Stores, Inc. (WMT) (in thousands)			
Revenue	1/31/2017	1/31/2016	1/31/2015
Total Revenue	485,873,000	482,130,000	485,651,000
Cost of Revenue	361,256,000	360,984,000	365,086,000
Gross Profit	**124,617,000**	**121,146,000**	**120,565,000**
Operating Expenses			
Selling General and Administrative	101,853,000	97,041,000	93,418,000
Operating Income or Loss	**22,764,000**	**24,105,000**	**27,147,000**
Income from Continuing Operations			
Total Other Income/Expenses Net	100,000	81,000	113,000
Earnings Before Interest and Taxes	22,864,000	24,186,000	27,260,000
Interest Expense	2,367,000	2,548,000	2,461,000
Income Before Tax	20,497,000	21,638,000	24,799,000
Income Tax Expense	6,204,000	6,558,000	7,985,000
Minority Interest	2,737,000	3,065,000	4,543,000
Net Income From Continuing Ops	**14,293,000**	**15,080,000**	**16,814,000**
Non-recurring Events			
Discontinued Operations	-	-	285,000
Net Income			
Net Income	**13,643,000**	**14,694,000**	**16,363,000**

The two most common kinds of expenses are the cost of goods sold (COGS) and selling general and administrative expenses (SG&A). The cost of goods sold represents the costs of production or services of a company.

SG&A includes expenses on marketing, utility bills, salaries, and various other general and administrative costs associated with a business. It includes depreciation and amortization as well. Some expenses, like research and development (R&D),

particularly at technology or pharmaceutical companies, are vital to future growth and should be adequate. You also need to consider taxes and interest payments.

Profit is equal to total revenue minus total expenses. Gross profit is revenue minus cost of sales. Companies having high gross profit margins are usually able to have more net profit. If the cost of goods sold rises, it might lower gross profit margins, unless the company passes these costs to the customers.

Operating profit is equal to revenue minus cost of sales and SG&A. It denotes the profit made from the actual operations. High operating margins imply that the company has effective control over the costs. Operating profit is a more reliable measure of the company's profitability as it is more difficult to manipulate with the various accounting tricks as compared to net profit.

Net profit represents a company's profit after all expenses have been paid. It is the net profit out of which you get the dividends.

You can get a lot of valuable insights about the company after analyzing its income statement, and consequently, about investing in the stock of the company.

Increasing sales are a great sign of the strong fundamentals of the business. Rising margins denote growing efficiency, and lead to higher profitability. If a company has high-profit margins, it usually implies that the company has some edge over its competition. A company with high net profit margins enjoys a large cushion to protect itself during business downturns.

Balance Sheet

The balance sheet reveals the financial condition of the company. It is also known as the statement of financial condition. It gives a snapshot of the financial condition of the company at a particular point in time.

Balance Sheet of Wal-Mart Stores, Inc. (WMT) (in thousands)			
Period Ending	1/31/2017	1/31/2016	1/31/2015
Current Assets			
Cash And Cash Equivalents	6,867,000	8,705,000	9,135,000
Net Receivables	5,835,000	5,624,000	6,778,000
Inventory	43,046,000	44,469,000	45,141,000
Other Current Assets	1,941,000	1,441,000	2,224,000
Total Current Assets	57,689,000	60,239,000	63,278,800
Property Plant and Equipment	114,178,000	116,516,000	116,655,000
Goodwill	17,037,000	16,695,000	18,102,000
Other Assets	9,921,000	6,131,000	5,455,000
Total Assets	198,825,000	199,581,000	203,490,000
Current Liabilities			
Accounts Payable	63,008,000	58,615,000	58,583,000
Short/Current Long Term Debt	3,920,000	6,004,000	6,670,000
Total Current Liabilities	66,928,000	64,619,000	65,253,000
Long Term Debt	42,018,000	44,030,000	43,495,000
Deferred Long Term Liability Charges	9,344,000	7,321,000	8,805,000
Minority Interest	2,737,000	3,065,000	4,543,000
Total Liabilities	121,027,000	119,035,000	122,096,000
Stockholders' Equity			
Common Stock	305,000	317,000	323,000
Retained Earnings	89,354,000	90,021,000	85,777,000
Capital Surplus	2,371,000	1,805,000	2,462,000
Other Stockholder Equity	-14,232,000	-11,597,000	-7,168,000
Total Stockholder Equity	77,798,000	80,546,000	81,394,000
Total Liabilities+Stockholders' Equity	198,825,000	199,581,000	203,490,000

Assets, liabilities, and stockholders' equity are the three key components of a balance sheet. It reveals the assets or how much the company owns; and the liabilities or how much it owes. The difference between the assets and the liabilities is net assets or the stockholders' equity.

The fundamental equation of the balance sheet balances the company's assets on the one hand and liabilities as well as the stockholders' equity on the other at a particular point in time, as shown below:

Assets = Liabilities + Stockholders' Equity

Assets show the total value of the resources that a company owns. The other side of the balance sheet equation shows the total value of liabilities and stockholders' equity, which finance the assets. Liabilities mainly denote debt, and equity shows the owners' contribution, including retained earnings out of the company's profits in previous years.

Assets

There are two types of assets, namely the current assets and the non-current assets. The existing assets are converted into cash or used up typically in a year or one operating cycle. The main current asset items include cash, inventories, and accounts receivables.

Inventories are the finished products made by the company that isn't sold yet. You need to assess whether a company has got too much money tied up in the inventory.

Receivables denote the outstanding or uncollected bills. The company's speed in collecting receivables indicates its financial efficiency.

Non-current assets include items such as property,

plant, and equipment (PP&E). Usually, the fixed assets are carried on the balance sheet at cost.

Liabilities

There are two types of liabilities, namely current liabilities and non-current liabilities. Current liabilities are the obligations that the company needs to pay within a year, such as accounts payable. Non-current liabilities refer to the obligations that the company needs to pay after at least a year, such as long-term bank debt.

Inventory turnover measures how quickly the company is moving merchandise through the warehouse to customers. It is calculated by dividing the cost of goods sold by average inventory.

Quick ratio is obtained by subtracting inventory from current assets and then dividing by current liabilities. If quick ratio is 1 or higher, it denotes the company has sufficient cash or liquid assets for paying out short-term obligations.

Quick Ratio =Current Assets - Inventories / Current Liabilities

Stockholders' Equity

There are two essential parts of stockholders' equity,

namely paid-in capital and retained earnings. Paid-in capital denotes money stockholders paid for the stocks when the company first offered the stock to the public. It simply means the money the firm received when it had first sold its stocks to the public. The retained earnings denote the money the company decided to reinvest in the business instead of paying a dividend to the stockholders.

Intangible Assets

Most of the companies have intangible assets, which include goodwill, brand value, and intellectual property items like trademarks, patents, copyrights. However, such assets are not usually shown on the company's balance sheet.

Off-balance Sheet Items

You also need to assess off-balance sheet items like debt. Off-balance sheet debt is a form of financing which involves keeping large capital expenditures off the company's balance sheet with the help of various classification methods. Companies undertake off-balance-sheet financing to show low levels of debt and give a reflection of a strong financial position.

Cash Flow Statement

The cash flow statement is a record of cash inflows and outflows of a company during a particular period of time.

Cash Flow Statement of Wal-Mart Stores, Inc. (WMT) (in thousands)			
Period Ending	1/31/2017	1/31/2016	1/31/2015
Net Income	13,643,000	14,694,000	16,363,000
Operating Activities, Cash Flows Provided By or Used In			
Depreciation	10,080,900	9,454,000	9,173,000
Adjustments To Net Income	967,000	738,000	-3,000
Changes In Accounts Receivables	-402,000	-19,000	-569,000
Changes In Liabilities	5,571,000	2,839,000	4,093,000
Changes In Inventories	1,021,000	-703,000	-1,229,000
Total Cash Flow From Operating Activities	31,530,000	27,389,000	28,564,000
Investing Activities, Cash Flows Provided By or Used In			
Capital Expenditures	-10,619,000	-11,477,000	-12,174,000
Investments	-4,364,000	-4,364,000	-4,364,000
Other Cash flows from Investing Activities	996,000	802,000	1,049,000
Total Cash Flows From Investing Activities	-13,987,000	-10,675,000	-11,125,000
Financing Activities, Cash Flows Provided By or Used In			
Dividends Paid	-6,695,000	-7,013,000	-6,785,000
Sale Purchase of Stock	-8,388,000	-5,438,000	-2,859,000
Net Borrowings	-3,591,000	-3,158,000	-5,018,000
Other Cash flows from Financing Activities	-255,000	-513,000	-409,000
Total Cash Flows From Financing Activities	-18,929,000	-16,122,000	-15,071,000
Effect Of Exchange Rate Changes	-452,000	-1,022,000	-514,000
Change In Cash and Cash Equivalents	-1,838,000	-430,000	1,854,000

The cash flow statement reveals how much cash a company gets and pays out over a period of time.

The cash flow statement is different from the income statement mainly due to accrual accounting, which is used for the income statement and records revenues and expenses when the particular transaction occurs instead of when cash is exchanged. Moreover, the cash flow statement never includes non-cash items, while the income statement includes some non-cash revenues or expenses.

The cash flow statement has three sections focusing on the three types of cash related activities:

Cash Flows from Operating Activities

These are the cash flows related to the day-to-day operations of the company. It shows cash flows from sales of the goods and services, net of the expenses incurred on selling.

You should usually invest in a company that has a net positive cash flow from operating activities. Some high growth firms, like new technology star-tups showing negative cash flow from operations, may prove to be good investments in the future.

You should become alert if you observe a widening gap between the reported earnings of a company and its cash flows from the operating activities.

If the net income of the company is much higher than its cash flows, the company may be aggressively booking its income or slowly booking its expenses wrongfully.

Cash Flows from Investing Activities

These are the cash flows related to the investing activities of the company such as cash outflows due to capital expenditures or investments in assets as well as the cash inflows from the sale of long-term assets

It shows the amount of cash that a company has spent on capital expenditures like a new plant, machinery, equipment, etc. It also includes the cash spent on investments like money market funds, the acquisition of a firm, etc.

You need to be aware that a good company needs to reinvest money in its business at least equal to the depreciation periodically. If a company is not reinvesting enough, it may show high cash inflows in the current period. Still, it is not sustainable, and the company may suffer in the future due to depreciating capital stock.

Cash Flow from Financing Activities

These are the cash flows related to the financing activities of the company. It reveals the sources of the inflows and outflows of cash associated with the outside financing activities.

Cash inflows come from selling stock, bank borrowings, issuing of bonds in the market for borrowing funds, etc. Cash outflows occur due to paying back a bank loan, dividend payments, redemptions of bonds, common stock repurchases, etc.

You can get some solid information regarding the financial position of the company by analyzing the cash flow statement, which is very difficult to manipulate as it relates to actual cash transactions.

Cash is critical. A company can get into trouble due to insufficient cash flows despite showing profit in income statements.

You should invest in the stock of a company that generates a good quantity of free cash flows (FCF), i.e., the excess cash after meeting the essential needs of the business.

Free cash flows provide a company the resources for paying dividends and debt, stock repurchases, and investing in growth opportunities and expansion.

Other relevant information

You can also access and analyze some other important information, which is relevant for your investment in the stocks of a company.

Management Discussion and Analysis (MD&A)

Management discussion and analysis (MD&A) provides details about what the company does. It is usually part of the annual report. It points out certain key areas and highlights the performance of the company. However, the analysis is at the management's discretion, so you cannot usually get any negatives in MD&A.

You can get clues about the performance and prospects of a company in managements' analysis, but you should first assess the candidness and accuracy of the management's comments.

If the management tries to avoid dealing with the issues clearly or confuse you with jargon and high sounding words, perhaps they may be hiding something. If a company gives additional and pertinent information in the MD&A, the management is most likely, to be honest.

The Auditor's Report

The auditor's report scrutinizes the company and identifies the issues, which may dent the integrity of the financial statements. An auditor expresses an opinion on the accuracy of the financial statements and whether they provide adequate disclosures.

The auditor's report gives credibility to the financial

statements and management reports. You should be cautious in investing in the stocks of a company whose financial statements have been flagged by an auditor.

The Notes to the Financial Statements

The notes to the financial statements provide important information that might not be included in the accounts, e.g., outstanding leases, maturity dates of debt, compensation plan details, stock options, and so on.

The footnotes explain the accounting policies adopted by the company and any changes therein.

You should be wary of investing in the stock if a company has changed its accounting policies. You need to assess whether the change in accounting policies was really needed or if the company is changing accounting policies only for taking advantage of current conditions or hiding its poor performance.

The footnotes also provide some additional disclosures which might not be given in the financial statements, e.g., pension plan liabilities, legal proceedings details, etc.

You can get all the financial statements and information from the annual report, website of the company, or even better from the relevant regulator of the companies in the country.

In the US, all publicly traded companies need to submit filings to the Securities and Exchange Commission (SEC). These filings, known as 10-K (annual) and 10-Q (quarterly), provide details about their financial activities. These filings also include all the three major financial statements along with other relevant information.

Insights from the Financial Statement Analysis for Investing in Stocks

You can get a lot of valuable insights about the company after analyzing its financial statements and, consequently, about investing in the stock of the company. You get to know how much debt the company has, what types of assets it has, how much cash it has, etc.

Increasing cash reserves indicates a strong company performance while decreasing cash reserves could be a sign of trouble.

If inventory grows faster than sales, it is almost always a sign of deteriorating fundamentals.

If the receivables collection period of a company is growing longer, you may take it as an indication of problems ahead.

If debt levels are falling, it's beneficial for the company as well as your investments in the stocks of the company. If a company has more assets as compared to its liabilities, then it is in a strong position.

Increasing sales are a grand sign of the strong fundamentals of the company.

Rising margins indicate increasing efficiency and lead to higher profitability.

If a company has high profit margins, it enjoys a huge cushion to protect itself during business downturns.

If a company has more debt with heavy interest and debt repayments, which are more than its cash flows required to pay them, the company has a great risk of going bankrupt.

PART: III - STRATEGIES TO WIN ON THE STOCK MARKET

11

INVESTMENT STYLES AND STRATEGIES

You may find it difficult to choose individual stocks from the global marketplace to analyze, buy, and thereafter track their performance. It is much more difficult in the context of a well-diversified portfolio.

One better and easier alternative is to make portfolio allocation decisions by choosing among the broad categories of stocks e.g., large-cap, mid-cap, value, growth, income, domestic, international, emerging markets, etc.

Style investing is an approach to investing that focuses on the underlying characteristics which are common to some particular types of investments.

Categorizing the stocks by style simplifies and crystallizes the investment choices. Allocating the investible funds among a limited number of investment styles is much easier as compared to choosing among the thousands of investment options.

You need to evaluate the performance of the portfolio relative to a performance benchmark for the specific style of investing.

Value Investing

Value investing style focuses on undervalued stocks as compared to the company's existing assets and earnings. It equates a stock's price to its intrinsic value. Value companies usually have relatively low price/earnings (PE) ratios, higher dividends payouts, relatively stable stock prices, etc.

The basic assumption of value investing is that the company's worth will be revalued at some point in time, providing substantial gains for the investments. Value investors look at the current earnings and assets of the stock.

There are several reasons for an undervaluation of a stock, including thinly traded stock of a small company, complicated corporate structure, the company is in an out-of-favor industry, etc. Value stocks are often found in the slow-growing sectors of the economy.

Traditional growth style investing now has got some sub-styles, like disciplined growth style, aggressive growth style, etc.

Deep Value Style

The deep value style is based on the traditional Graham and Dodd investing approach. Here, the investor buys the cheapest stocks and holds them for a long time in anticipation of a good market upswing.

Relative Value Style

The relative value style focuses on the stocks that are undervalued relative to the market, peer group, as well as the company's earnings potential. These stocks also have something big in store like a pending patent, which may cause an upswing in the value of the stock. Investors tap relative value opportunities in all sectors and hold a relative value stock usually for a three to five year period.

New Value Style

Investors choose any stock that has a high prospect for considerable price appreciation from all sectors.

Growth Investing

The growth style investors focus on a company's future earnings potential. They try to spot the stocks which offer a high potential for earnings growth at above the average rates.

Growth investors look at the future earnings potential of the stock. Growth style investing has greater downside risk as well.

Traditional growth style investing now has got some sub-styles like disciplined growth style, aggressive growth style, etc.

Disciplined Growth Style

The disciplined growth style focus on the stocks with high potential for an increase in the earnings at an above averages rate and the stock is available for a reasonable price.

Aggressive Growth Style

The aggressive growth style focuses on technical analysis instead of the traditional valuation methods or the fundamental analysis. It is also known as momentum style.

Income Investing

The income investing style focuses on the stocks that provide income to the investors consistently. It chooses the stocks that have a good performance history with dividend payments on a regular basis.

Dividend Investing

The dividend investing strategy focuses on buying stocks with a strong track record of earnings and dividends. This helps in getting a regular payout from the stocks. You'll get some regular income regardless of the decline in the market price of the stock. If you are a retiree, it is one of the best strategies for supplementing your income.

Sector Strategy

It focuses on investing in a particular sector or industry, such as information technology. It is high risk and high reward strategy and lacks diversification. It gets high-value increases in the portfolio based on large stock price upswings in case of increased demand for the product or services of the chosen sector. However, in case of a downturn in the selected sector, it experiences hefty losses owing to concentrated investment holdings.

Index Strategy

This is a passive investing style. It tracks an index like the S&P 500, with the portfolio having the same type of securities with the same weights. It has a low management expense ratio. Historically, many funds have failed to surpass the returns of a broad index like the S&P 500.

Global Strategy

This focuses on building a diversified portfolio of stocks from any country across the globe. Global portfolios may also focus on a particular sector or style. The investments may be allocated with the weights in accordance with the world market capitalization weights.

Stable Value Strategy

This is a conservative investment strategy. It focuses on the short-term fixed-income securities with almost guaranteed returns and protection from the price volatility due to interest rate movements.

Dollar-Cost Averaging

Dollar-Cost averaging is a traditional investing strategy based on investing a specific fixed dollar amount in stocks at regular time intervals. In case of price declines, you buy a larger number of stocks for your fixed investment amount and a smaller number in case of a stock price increase. Thus, the average cost of stocks becomes reasonable, moderating the large price fluctuations.

Value Averaging

Value averaging is based on adjusting the total investment amount to meet a fixed target. For example, you want to invest in a fund with a value of $100 per month. In the second month, you invest $110 in case your initial first-month investment of $100 has declined to $90, or you invest $95 in case initial investment increased to $105, or you invest the same $100 in case of the price being stable.

Thus, at the end of the second month, your total investment in the fund is $200 at the current stock value. So, you invest more money when stock prices are down; and less money when stock prices are up.

You should choose a style or strategy for stock investing after a comprehensive and thoughtful analysis. Thereafter, you should stick to the selected style or strategy for a reasonable time, so that it can bear fruit. While deciding your investment style and strategy, you should consider various factors such as your risk appetite, investment time horizon, income levels, liquidity needs, etc.

12

VALUE INVESTING

The value investing strategy focuses on identifying and picking the stocks that are currently available in the market at a price that is less than their intrinsic value. Value investors actively search for undervalued stocks.

Value investing is rigorously focused on the here and now. It zeros in on the stocks which are currently trading for a lesser amount of their apparent worth in terms of lower price-to-sales (P/S) ratio, price-to-book (P/B) ratio, industry average price-to-earnings (P/E) ratio, etc.

Value investing advocates picking stocks that are trading below their appropriate valuation mark due to some temporal reasons like bad quarterly results, adverse events affecting a company, rejection of a patent, a big fine imposed on the company, etc. As these temporal reasons would change in the near future, the stock would achieve its true value in the stock market, and the value investors would be able to make much profit.

Value investing is based on the premise that the stock markets often overreact to various good and bad news as well as company-related happenings. This results in price movements of stocks that are out of sync with the company's future earning potential and long-term fundamentals. A value investor capitalizes on the mispricing of the stock by the market and buys a stock when its price is deflated.

Undervalued stocks are an outcome of investing irrationality. A value investor tries to profit from this irrationality by selecting and buying these undervalued stocks in large quantities.

A value stock is a stock that is trading in the market at a lesser price relative to the fundamentals like sales, earnings, or dividends. The undervalued stock is available in the market at a price which is lower than its price to book ratio or lower than the average price to earnings ratios in its industry.

Such stocks usually tend to have high dividend yields.

A value investor compares these ratios and numbers with the intrinsic value of the stock. The value investor makes investments in the stock if the comparative ratios or valuation are favorable.

The intrinsic value refers to the perceived or computed value of a stock based on the future earnings, cash flows, or some other attribute.

Benjamin Graham is known as the father of value investing. He propounded that any investment or stock should be worth much more than what you are paying for it. If it is not so, you should not invest in it. He advised that you should invest in companies with strong balance sheets, high-profit margins, low debt, etc.

There are certain drawbacks related to value investing. The estimation of the intrinsic value of the stock is complex and difficult. Therefore, it is crucial that you have an adequate margin of safety when you apply this strategy. A value investor needs to buy a stock at a significant discount to accommodate errors in the estimation of stock value.

The value investing strategy is subjective. Most of

the value investors focus only on the present assets and earnings but ignore future growth potential. The most basic logic of value investing is an essential economic concept. It ordains that you should buy something for less than its current worth.

13

GROWTH INVESTING

Growth investing is an investment style focused on the capital appreciation or price increase of the stocks. Growth investors invest in companies that show potential for high growth even if their stock price seems to be expensive.

Thomas Rowe Price Jr. is considered the father of growth investing. Phil Fisher popularized this investment style with his seminal 1958 book "Common Stocks and Uncommon Profits" - a great reference for identifying growth companies even today.

Growth investing focuses more on the future potential of a company rather than its present price. The growth investors are willing to buy the stocks of the companies which are currently trading at higher than their current intrinsic worth but have substantial future growth potential. They think that the intrinsic value of the company will further grow and exceed even their current rich valuations by a significant margin.

Generally, investors that are using this method focuses on the young and new companies, particularly in the swiftly expanding industries or new technology-based sectors.

Growth investing underlines the belief that high growth in the revenues and earnings will directly lead to an increase in the price of the stock. You realize the profits through capital gains or increase in the price of the stock; and not through the dividends because most growth companies do not pay dividends, instead they tend to reinvest their earnings for expansion.

The growth investing style produced enormous returns for the stock investors in the late 1990s when many technology companies were thriving, and thus became very popular.

However, the bust of the dotcom bubble led to huge losses to many growth investors who invested in the seemingly high growth technology companies having only high sounding promises and few strong fundamentals. Naturally, growth investing comes with high levels of risk, but can also yield great returns.

A company that is developing new technologies or creating innovations is an excellent choice for growth investors. The stock of a company that develops a revolutionary product can show an exponential rise in price in a short time. For instance, the stock price of Pfizer was just under $5 in 1994. Once, the Viagra was released and it became a blockbuster drug, it took the stock price of Pfizer to above $30 in the next five years.

A prime target of the growth investors is the small-cap companies often defined as companies with their market capitalization being in the range of $300 million to $2 billion. Companies in this category are often in their initial growth phase. Their stocks have a high potential for considerable capital appreciation. Many small-cap stocks have posted historically higher returns as compared to the blue-chip companies. However, small-cap stocks are also significantly much more volatile and have a much higher level of risk.

14

INCOME INVESTING

Income investing is an investment style that seeks a regular income stream from the investments. Using this strategy is to pick the stocks that have a good performance history and consistent dividend payments.

Income investing is a straightforward stock-picking strategy.

Income investing targets established companies of a specific size with a history of regular dividend payments. Such companies are generally in an industry that is no longer in a rapidly expanding phase. These companies tend to pay out the earnings as dividends to the investors as a return instead of reinvesting the earnings. One good example is Johnson & Johnson.

Dividend Yield

Income investing is not merely about the investment in the companies paying the highest dividends in absolute terms in the dollar figures. A better return metric is the dividend yield. The dividend yield is calculated by dividing the annual dividend paid per stock by the current stock price. It measures the actual return on investment which a stockholder gets.

For example, if company A pays out a dividend of $10, and company B pays a dividend of $6, it seems like company A is the obvious choice.

However, if you analyze the company some more, the picture changes. The current market price of the stock of company A is $200, but the current market price of the stock of company B is $60.

This means that the dividend yield of the stock of company A is 5%, but the dividend yield of the stock of company B is 10%. In other words, the appropriate choice for an income investor would be company B. Income investors usually look for a yield of 5% at least.

The main principle underlying the income strategy is to find the companies providing high dividend yields on a sustainable basis to get a predictable and steady stream of income over a long time.

You should also examine the dividend policy and the history of dividend payments of a company. You must assess whether the company can continue its dividends on a sustainable basis for the foreseeable period of time. The longer a company has been able to pay out dividends, the better. However, you should not invest in a stock solely based on the company's dividend payments. A company that has paid high dividends for some years is not necessarily fundamentally strong. Dividends are paid out of a company's net profit, and consequently, higher dividends would lead to lower retained earnings. This means that less money can be used for future expansion. It is very much important that the dividend yield of a stock is sustainable.

15

STOCK MARKET TIPS & TRICKS

You need to understand and realize a couple of things regarding stock investing. First of all, there is no sure-shot formula for profitable stock investing. Even the most successful and celebrated investors lose money in some cases.

However, there are some rules that are followed by many successful stock investors. These rules prove to be useful over a long period and a sufficient number of stock trades.

Hereunder, you will find some excellent tips. If you follow them prudently and take into account the specifics of a particular stock or market condition, you may increase the chances of a good return on your investments.

Tips & Tricks - Do's

- You should have a long-term approach to stock investing with a broad picture of your investment goals in your mind.
- You need to have a thoroughly grounded and realistic perspective. Making money in stocks is not an easy task. Learning to invest doesn't happen overnight. It takes time and effort to become successful at it. Persistence is vital when learning to invest. Don't get discouraged.
- As a new investor, be prepared to take some small losses. Experience is a great teacher.
- You'll need to do much research and develop a sound understanding of the stock market before getting starting.
- You should follow a well-disciplined investment approach. If you put in money systematically in the right stocks and hold on to your investments for a sufficient period, you would increase your chances of generating good returns.
- You should always make an informed decision. Do a proper analysis of the

fundamentals of a stock before investing in that particular stock.

- You should create a well-diversified portfolio by investing in several good stocks of well-known companies with leadership positions in their industries. Diversification will reduce your risks and heavy losses.
- You should invest in the right stocks or companies. Strong sales and earnings growth characterize these as well as increasing or good profit margins, consistent and high return on equity of 15% or more, industry leader or with large market share, etc.
- You should have realistic expectations. In times of bull runs, some stocks generated returns of 25% plus. However, you cannot take such a performance as your annual benchmark return for your stock investment. It may lead you to take unnecessary risks. You should aim for a return of 10%.
- You should monitor your stock investments or portfolio regularly and rigorously. This will help you in making desired changes in

your portfolio with the evolving market conditions. Concentrate your eggs in a few solid baskets, know each of them well, and keep on watching them vigilantly.

- You should learn from the great investors. It is advised to never invest in the stock but to invest in the business. You should invest in a business or market that you understand. This will help you in judging the proper value of a company and its stock and consequently increase your chances of identifying good stocks for profitable investing.

- It is also important to pick the right broker with a good track record, online facilities, tools and apps, high-grade customer support, etc.

Tips & Tricks - Don'ts

- At least in the beginning, do not invest in companies or sectors that are characterized by much volatility or fluctuations in stock prices.

- As a beginner, do not set up a margin account; but set up a cash account.

- You should avoid more volatile types of investments, at least in the initial phase, like futures, options, and foreign stocks.

- You should not buy a stock just because it is cheap. You generally get what you pay for in the market. Cheaply priced stocks are usually cheap for a reason

- You should avoid the herd mentality and invest in a particular stock because your friends, relatives, or acquaintances are buying the stock. Always invest in a stock after you do your own research and once understand the fundamentals of that stock.

- You should not try to time the stock market. Catching the top or the bottom of the stock market is not a good idea. You may lose money in trying to time the market.

- Do not allow your emotions and sentiments to cloud your judgment regarding stock investments. Many investors have lost money, mainly due to their failure to control their emotions. These emotions are usually fear and greed.

- You should never speculate by building heavy positions in some stocks, buying stocks of unknown companies, etc. The fabulous dream to become a millionaire overnight may even wipe out your hard-earned money.

PART: IV - ADVANCE STOCK MARKET STRATEGIES AND TACTICS

16

SHORT SELLING

Short selling is the sale of a stock that is not owned by the seller. You may borrow the stock from some other investor or a broker.

Short selling is based on the perception that the price of a stock would decline in the near future. You can buy the same stock which you have short at a higher price, at a lower price later. You would be able to make a good profit by short selling if things occur as you thought.

You may do short selling for speculation. You may also do short selling for hedging the downside risk of your long position in a stock.

However, it is better for you to avoid short selling until you've acquired more experience in stock trading. This is simple logic because a short sale has a theoretically infinite risk of loss due to the fact that a stock may rise to any price level.

For example, you believe that the stock XYZ, which is trading at $20, will decline in price. You borrow 50 stocks and sell them. You are now "short" 50 stocks of XYZ as you sold a stock that you did not own. Your short sale was made possible through borrowing the stocks from another investor or your brokerage.

After 10 days, the price of XYZ falls to $10 due to poor quarterly results. You can now buy the 50 stocks, give them back to the owner, and make a profit of $500. You may have to pay commissions or interest on the margin account out of your profit of $500.

But if the price of XYZ rises to $40, you will incur a loss of $1000.

You have to take care of the two metrics while short selling. Short interest is the total number of stocks sold short as a percentage of the total outstanding stocks of a company. Short interest ratio (SIR) is the total number of stocks sold short divided by the average daily trading volume of the stock.

You also face a risk of buy-in. The brokerage, you borrowed stock from, may close out your short position at any time if it feels that the stock is hard to borrow or the lenders want it back.

Short selling is often disparaged for its speculative nature; however, it has some good aspects as well. Short selling gives liquidity to the stock markets. It also prevents stocks from rising to very high price levels on hype. Short selling may be a good tool for risk management.

17

BUYING ON MARGIN

Buying on margin is purchasing stocks by paying the margin i.e., a part of the total purchase price of the stocks. You can borrow the balance from your broker.

You need to make an initial payment to the broker for buying the stocks on margin. You need to give the collateral for your borrowed funds, and the stocks in your account with the broker serve as the marginal securities. You'll need to open a margin account with a broker who provides the facility to buy on margin to get started.

You need to fund at least 50% of the purchase price of a stock with cash. You can borrow the remaining from your broker.

Your broker sets an initial margin, and you fund the initial margin in your account before you can begin buying on margin. You need to keep some maintenance margins as well in your account.

The maintenance margin denotes the minimum amount of funds you must keep in your account. If your funds in the account fall below the maintenance margin, your broker may force you to deposit more money.

Buying on margin gives you some benefits. You can buy more stocks by leveraging borrowed money from others. You can amplify your gains when the value of your purchased stocks increases.

Buying on margin has a lot of risks as well. When you buy on margin and the value of your stocks fall, you would need more money to fund the margin requirements of your account with the broker. If you are not able to fund the margin, then your broker may close out your position. Thus, you may have to bear more losses due to the sudden selling of the stocks in a falling market. So your losses are magnified when the price of your stocks decline in value.

A margin call occurs when the funds in your

brokerage account fall below the maintenance margin. Your broker calls you and demands that you bring the balance in the account back to the required maintenance margin level. You can do this by depositing additional cash into your brokerage account or, you can sell some of the stocks that you purchased with the borrowed money.

For example, you buy 1000 stocks of company ABC at $10 per stock. You deposit $5000 and borrow $5000 from your broker. After 2 years, the stock price doubles to $20. You sell stocks for $20,000 and pay back your broker the $5000. You triple your money and make $15000 on a $5000 investment. This is leveraging someone else's assets.

If the price of the stock falls to $5, you sell the stocks for $5000. You pay this back to your broker. Thus, you lose all your money owing to buying on margin.

18

DAY TRADING

D ay trading refers to the buying and selling of stocks within the same day. As a day trader, you may engage in buying and selling of stocks multiple times during the course of a single day.

Day trading aims to take benefit of the small movements in the price of the stocks. It is always hectic and stressful whether you're making profits or incurring losses.

Day trading is a dangerous style of stock trading, particularly for those who are new to the game or for those who are overwhelmed by emotions and don't stick to a well thought out strategy.

Day traders make money from minute price movements in individual stocks. They often leverage vast amounts of funds to exploit price differences.

Day Trading Parameters

You need to take care of the three parameters: liquidity, volatility, and trading volume.

Liquidity indicates the ease of doing a transaction in the stocks. High liquidity facilitates your trades.

Volatility is a measure of the anticipated daily price range of a stock. High volatility means large profit or loss.

Trading volume indicates the total number of trades for a particular stock in a day. A large daily volume is an indication of a high level of interest in a particular stock.

Scalping is a popular day trading strategy. You sell almost immediately after your trade becomes profitable. The price target is a price which is higher than your purchase price plus any transaction cost.

Momentum is another popular day trading strategy. You trade based on some news releases or events related to the stock. You buy on the news releases indicating some positives for the stock and then ride the trend until it shows signs of reversal.

Day Trading Tips

- Acquire knowledge of proper trading procedures, the latest news of events that affect stocks, stock market trends, etc.
- Fix an amount for day trading, i.e., usually 1-2% of your total investment funds
- Start on a small scale with trades involving a small amount of money.
- Avoid penny stocks.
- Start with the middle hours of a trading day, which are less volatile usually.
- Use Limit Orders for controlling losses.
- Control your emotions during trading hours.
- Chalk out an elaborate plan or well-defined strategy and follow the same with discipline.

Day trading is a challenging skill and requires a lot of time, effort, and discipline. Most of the people who try it fail and some fail miserably. You should always follow one rule: Set and strictly follow a maximum loss limit for a trading day, which you can afford without financial distress.

19

ONLINE TRADING

Online trading is buying and selling stocks through an internet-based trading platform. The online trading platforms are usually proprietary and generally belong to the brokerages. It is also known as e-trading.

Online trading has increased by leaps and bounds since the early 2000s, especially with the introduction of powerful computers and high-speed internet connections. Nowadays, many investors use online trading platforms for investing on their own.

You can have many facilities on online trading platforms. You get multiple tools for trading and investing. You can place, buy, and sell orders for various stocks. You can place multiple types of orders, like market order, limit order, stop-loss, etc.

You can check the status of your order in real-time. You can also view the real-time quotes for various stocks. Some of the online trading platforms give you an excellent dashboard with various facilities and tools for tracking your investment portfolio, checking transaction history, etc.

Many brokerages that have an affiliation with the banks provide you the added convenience by linking your bank account with your investment account. This allows you to do transfers between your accounts easily.

Online trading has dramatically reduced the costs of trading. Most of the brokers have also lowered the commission for trading online.

Online trading with lower fees has helped many people get started in stock investing. The brokers have ramped up their online trading platforms with automated trading. This way, they save much money that would have been spent on human resources.

You can benefit from online trading in terms of the high speed of execution of transactions since no paperwork is needed.

Before opening an online trading account with a broker, you should check the broker's past track record, tools, and facilities offered, etc.

You should also be aware that all types of stocks are not available for online trading. For example, you may not be able to trade a stock online, that is trading on the pink sheets or over-the-counter market. If you want to place an order for such a stock, you need to call your broker and hand over the task.

20

PORTFOLIO MANAGEMENT

Portfolio management is the process of investing in various types of financial instruments such as stocks, bonds, mutual funds, fixed deposits, etc. to create a diversified basket for meeting your investment objectives.

It emphasizes on the selection of the right type of stocks which meets your risk-return objectives and give you the optimum returns on your investments.

The fundamental principle of portfolio management is the minimum risk and maximum return, keeping in view your investment requirements and constraints.

Asset allocation is the key element of portfolio management. Asset allocation is based on the long-term mix of assets. Different types of financial assets are not the same - some are volatile; others are stable. Asset allocation helps in optimizing the risk-return profile through investments in different assets with a low correlation between them.

If you want an aggressive profile, you can invest more in stocks. If you want a conservative profile, you can invest more in stable assets like bonds.

Portfolio Management Objectives

Portfolio management may have the following objectives based on your expectations and requirements:

- Capital Appreciation
- Consistent Returns
- Preservation of Principal Amount Invested
- Marketability of Stocks
- Liquidity
- Risk Diversification
- Tax Planning

Portfolio Management Process

The portfolio management process is a continuous

and regular activity. You should optimize your investments to the pre-determined objectives. You should do the rebalancing of your portfolio in view of the evolving conditions for better risk and return balance.

You'd better have a well-defined investment policy for achieving your portfolio goals.

You should change your asset allocation periodically based on portfolio performance and the performance of various stocks in your portfolio.

Portfolio management is crucial as it helps in selecting the best investment strategy based on income, risk-taking capacity, funds availability, age, etc. You can keep an eye on the risk taken while investing.

Types of Portfolio Management

Active portfolio management refers to the active management of the buy-sell transactions of stocks for fulfilling investment objectives.

Passive portfolio management refers to the tracking of a market index for investing in stocks.

Discretionary portfolio management denotes a situation in which you allow a professional to manage your stock portfolio and to make financial decisions on your behalf.

Non-discretionary portfolio management refers to a situation where the portfolio manager has an advisory role, and you make the decisions.

PART: V - STOCK MARKET PRACTICAL LESSONS

STOCK BROKERS

You need to have a brokerage account to start investing in stocks. You need to consider a number of things while choosing your broker. You should be careful because all brokers are not appropriate for your particular needs.

There are two types of brokers for you. The first one is regular brokers who deal with you directly. Another type is broker-reseller who acts as an intermediary between you and a large regular broker. Regular brokers are usually better in terms of many parameters.

There is one more classification of brokers - full-service brokers and discount brokers. The full-service brokers give you many services like research, individualized suggestions, one-on-one advice, etc. but they have more expensive. The discount brokers charge less but offer limited and main services like the execution of your stock trade orders, basic customer services, etc.

For new investors, discount brokers are good enough to begin with. Moreover, in the beginning, you might have a limited pool of investible funds, so the cost per stock traded would be much higher in your case if you take the services of a full-service broker.

Following needs to be considered when choosing a broker:

- Fast execution of your trades, particularly during peak trading hours.
- Multiple options to place orders like online trade, orders through customer executive, fax orders, telephone trade, etc.
- Low fees.
- Require fewer minimum deposits for opening an investment account.
- A broker that offers customer service and help.

- A broker that offers the best rate on your cash deposits.

You should choose a broker as per your individual investment needs. If you are going to do more trades, choose a broker with low execution fees. If you are going to make long-term investments and have significant investible funds, you may choose a full-service broker providing excellent research and one-to-one advice.

SUCCESSFUL STOCK MARKET INVESTORS

M any individuals have been extremely successful in stock market investing. There are many influential names, for example, Warren Buffett, a man who is celebrated around the world. Many investors try to emulate the successful ones and experience positive results.

The successful stock market investors have some common traits and solid strategies that have helped them in being successful.

The investors below might be a good source for you to get inspired and acquire some wisdom from.

Warren Buffett

Warren Buffett is considered to be the greatest

investor in the world. He is also known as the Oracle of Omaha for his wisdom. He has been investing successfully for many decades, consistently.

His holdings company Berkshire Hathaway has an amazing record of creating wealth for the investors. An investment of $10,000 in Berkshire Hathaway that was made in 1965 is today worth about $50 million. Many investors around the world follow Buffet for his investing wisdom and tips.

He has a great ability to pick the best stocks. His investment philosophy is value investing. He picks stocks that are available at a price that is less than their intrinsic value. He prefers to invest in great businesses for the long-term with patience and discipline.

John Templeton

Templeton is the pioneer of the global mutual fund industry. He founded the investment fund Templeton Growth Ltd in 1954. He earned billions by introducing globally diversified mutual funds.

He was declared 'arguably the greatest global stock picker of the century' by Money Magazine in 1999. He advised buy low and sell high, to be bold, and to pay attention to the companies that other investors ignore.

Peter Lynch

Lynch managed the Fidelity Magellan Fund from 1977 to 1990. He increased its assets from $20 million to $14 billion, with an annual average return of 29% beating the S&P 500 Index benchmark in 11 of the 13 years.

Peter Lynch adapted strategies and styles based on the situation and what would work best at any given time. His writings "One Up on Wall Street", and "Beating the Street" gives great investing advice to the investors.

He advised that you should invest in what you know, due diligence before investing, focusing on a company's fundamentals, investing for the long run, paying little attention to short-term market fluctuations, etc.

John C Bogle

He pioneered low-cost index investing by founding the Vanguard Group in 1974. He led it to become the second largest mutual fund company in the world. He created Vanguard 500, the first index fund.

Bogle favored a broadly diversified portfolio made up of low-cost index funds, no-load, low-cost, low-turnover, and passively managed. He advised: diversification, low cost investing, long-term holding, and not to time the market.

George Soros

George Soros started his life as a railroad porter and a restaurant waiter. After graduating from the London School of Economics in 1952, he worked with an investment bank. Soros immigrated to the US in 1956 and started working as a trader and analyst.

Soros set up a private investment firm in 1973, which ultimately became the Quantum Fund. Over time, Soros amassed a fortune through his excellent investments.

He was a short-term speculator. He made huge and successful bets on the direction of financial markets. He ran his hedge fund for two decades, with returns of over 30% and over 100% in 2 years. He advised research and capitalizing on macro trends.

Carl Icahn

Carl Icahn is one of the greatest private equity investors. He founded Icahn & Co. in 1968, a securities firm with a focus on risk arbitrage and options trading.

He has earned billions from investments in real estate, food packaging, metals, gaming, etc. Many investors started investing in the companies in which Carl had invested in. Whenever Icahn begins to invest in a company, the company gets "Icahn Lift," i.e., a quick rise in its stock price.

His strategy is to get on the board of companies he invests in and improve their performance. Otherwise, he breaks it up and sells off profitably.

There are numerous other highly successful stock investors. You can learn a lot by studying their investing careers and apply the knowledge you have gathered to your own investments.

STOCK MARKET GURUS

There are a number of persons who have shaped the stock market discipline. There are some very prominent names like Benjamin Graham, Philip Fisher, etc. They have a cult status. Millions of investors follow the teachings and guidelines of these stock market gurus.

Benjamin Graham

Ben Graham is acknowledged as the father of two fundamental investment disciplines viz. value investing and security analysis.

His book "Security Analysis", published in 1934, is the bible for investors.

His second book, "The Intelligent Investor", was

published in 1949. According to Warren Buffett, it is the best book ever written about investing.

He says that your investments should be worth much more than what you pay for them. He focused on fundamental analysis. He advised investing in companies with strong balance sheets, above-average profit margins, little debt, ample cash flows, etc.

His ideas and investment teachings have mentored millions of investors around the world.

Philip Fisher

Fisher is considered the father of growth investing. Fisher wrote several books on investment strategies. His book "Common Stocks and Uncommon Profits" was the first investment book to make to the New York Times Best Sellers List.

He advised investing in companies with high growth potential, long-term investing, gathering and analyzing information, focus on a few stocks, etc.

Thomas Rowe Price, Jr.

Price founded T Rowe Price in 1937. Price developed the growth stock style of investing.

He advised fundamental research for investing, focus on individual stock picking for long-term, diversification, discipline, investing in well-managed companies, etc.

Apart from these three pioneers of investment philosophies, there many other stock market gurus. There is very much that you can learn from these.

STOCK MARKET AND INVESTMENT BOOKS

There are many books written on the topic of stock investing. Some of them are musts for any investor. There are a lot of principles and concepts, which are needed to be understood well for making profitable investments in the stocks.

Note: I am not an affiliate to the books listed down below. I make no money referring you to these materials. The only point of sharing these is to help you succeed.

Down below is a list of related book you could benefit from:

The Intelligent Investor

The Intelligent Investor, written by Benjamin Graham, the father of value investing, is the book that leads all charts on investment books. It has sold over 1 million copies. It describes value investing and stock market success.

Security Analysis

Security Analysis, also written by Benjamin Graham, is a must-read for learning more about the basics of the stock market. It helps you understand the discipline of analyzing stocks.

Common Stocks and Uncommon Profits

Written by Philip Fisher, the father of growth investing, this book will teach you a lot about stock investing and analyzing a company.

One Up On Wall Street

Written by Peter Lynch, this book explains in a lucid manner how you can find good stocks that have a high potential for growth and price increase.

The Little Book of Common Sense Investing

This book was written by Jack Bogle, the founder of The Vanguard Group. It explains stock market investing in a very simple manner. It advises you to keep costs low and invest in the market indexes for the long run.

Alchemy of Finance

Written by George Soros, this thought-provoking book will deepen your understanding of how financial markets work.

Buffett: The Making of an American Capitalist

This book by Roger Lowenstein will give you insights into the methods of investing practiced by Warren Buffett. You can learn a lot about the successful investment strategies and their application.

Irrational Exuberance

The 2013 Nobel Prize winner in economics Robert Shiller wrote this book to broaden our understanding of the markets and their movements. It explains macro trends, booms, busts, and business cycles.

The Age of Turbulence

This book, written by Alan Greenspan, the former Fed chairman, will enhance your understanding of the US economy in the last 50 years and the future scenarios.

How to Make Money in Stocks

This classic written by William O'Neil describes ins and outs of investing, finding stock market winners, how to time entries and exits, etc. This book combines both fundamental and technical analysis.

There are many other books, classic as well as the newly written ones which you can read to enhance your knowledge of stock markets and learn some good tips and tricks for profitable stock investing.

STOCK MARKET TERMINOLOGY

Knowing the most common terms in this field can enhance your understanding and benefit you over the long-term in stock investing. Down below is a list of terms worth keeping in mind when trying to learn more about investing.

Ask: The price of a stock that a seller is ready to take. It denotes how much a stock would cost.

Assets: Everything the company owns, including cash, land, etc.

Backtesting: Applying a strategy to similar historical data to test if it is valid.

Bear market: A period of declining stock prices.

Beta: A measure of the relationship between the price of a stock and market movement.

Block trade: Buying or selling many stocks.

Bull market: A period of rising stock prices.

Bid: The price of a stock that a buyer is ready to pay. It denotes how much you would get when you sell a stock.

Close: The price of a stock at the end of a trading day.

Defensive stock: A stock that gives dividends and earnings even in economic downturns.

Dividend: A payment made by a company to the stockholders.

Dow Jones industrial average: A stock market index averaging the value of 30 component stocks.

Earnings Per Stock (EPS): The profit of a company divided by the number of outstanding stocks.

Ex-dividend date: Date on which the buyer of a stock would not be entitled to the upcoming dividend.

Fundamental analysis: Analysis of the financial position of a company to assess the stock price.

Income stock: A stock with a good record of dividend payments

Hedge: Limiting your losses or reducing risk by placing orders to cover two or more possible events in the market

Initial Public Offering (IPO): First issue of stocks by a company to the public.

Limit order: An order to buy or sell a stock at a specific price.

Liquidity: Ability to sell or buy a stock without affecting its price.

Margin: Borrowing money for trading more stocks than possible with your own funds.

Margin Call: A call to replenish funds in your account when funds in your account fall below the minimum margin requirement.

Market capitalization: The total value of a company's outstanding stocks. It is calculated by multiplying the total number of stocks by the price of the stock.

Market order: Order for buying or selling a particular stock at its current market price

Moving average: It is the average of the cost of a stock over a period.

Price-to-Earnings Ratio (P/E Ratio): The stock price divided by earnings per stock (EPS) of a company.

Quote: The bid or ask price for a stock.

Short sale: Selling stocks without owning, usually through borrowing from the broker.

Spread: Difference between the bid and ask price of a stock.

Stop order: Buying or selling a stock after it reaches a specific price.

Technical analysis: Analysis of price trends of a stock on the basis of charts and market data.

Volatility: Change in the price of a stock over a period of time.

Volume: Quantity of stocks being traded at a time.

Yield: It is the measure of return on stock investment as a percentage of a stock's price.

FINAL WORDS

Stock market investing can be very powerful for any person looking to create wealth or build a side income. Among all the asset classes, stock investments have generated the best returns historically. Consequently, it is beneficial for you over the long term that you develop a sound understanding of this highly profitable investment avenue.

You should understand the fundamentals of the stock market, economy, asset classes, asset allocation, risks involved, your investment objectives, etc. You can use mutual funds, exchange-traded funds and IPOs for profitable investments. A broad-based mutual fund gives you an opportunity to earn good returns with low risk. All these have been discussed in lesson 1 to 5 lucidly.

All the successful investors advise that you should invest in what you know; therefore, it is necessary that you do thorough research and analysis of the industry and company in which you are going to invest. You need to understand the fundamental financial statement analysis to assess the value of a stock. All of these topics, along with basic fundamental analysis techniques, have been explained in detail in lesson 6 to 10.

There are a number of investment styles and strategies which you can use to make profitable investments in stocks. Value investing emphasize that you should invest in the stocks which are available at a price lower than their intrinsic value. The growth investing strategy advises that you should invest in companies with high future growth potential, even if you have to pay more to buy such stocks.

You can follow the income investing strategy to earn a regular income by investing in the companies with solid dividend payment track record. All these investment strategies, together with stock market tips, have been elaborated in lesson 11 to 15.

You can also use some high return high-risk strategies and techniques to enhance your profits from stock market investments like short selling, buying on margin, day trading, etc. You can use online trading for low cost and convenient stock investing. Portfolio management is required for risk diversification by spreading investments across various sectors and companies. All these have been discussed in lesson 16 to 20.

You need to select a good broker to invest in stocks, keeping in view the cost of transactions and facilities offered. You can learn a lot from successful investors like Warren Buffet, who has made billions from stock investing. Stock market gurus like Ben Graham, Fisher; as well as top investment books like "The Intelligent Investor" can illuminate the difficult path of stock investing. All of these are given in detail in the lesson 21 to 25.

Stock investing requires discipline, patience, and thoughtful analysis. Diversification is an essential strategy for successful stock investing. Keeping your emotions in check is also a crucial part of becoming a successful investor. A long-term approach to stock investments provides many times good returns.

Thank you for purchasing this book. By reading it to the end, you are proving that you are disciplined and ready to work hard! Many rookie investors spend their money investing blindly. Unlike the majority, you have taken your time to acquire knowledge to make wise decisions. Good job!

Finally, if you received any value or enjoyed reading this book, a review on Amazon would be appreciated.

Good luck!

Printed in Great Britain
by Amazon

56603044R00097